W9-BAG-201

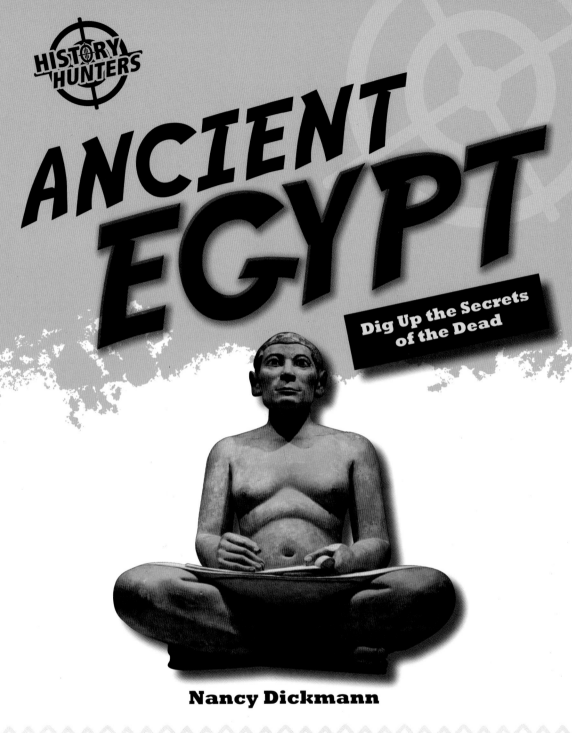

HISTORY HUNTERS

ANCIENT EGYPT

Dig Up the Secrets of the Dead

Nancy Dickmann

CAPSTONE PRESS
a capstone imprint

To contact Capstone Global Library please call 800-747-4992, or visit our web site
www.capstonepub.com

Produced for Capstone by Calcium
Edited by Sarah Eason and Jennifer Sanderson
Designed by Paul Myerscough
Picture research by Rachel Blount
Consultant: John Malam
Production by Paul Myerscough
Originated by Calcium Creative Limited © 2016
Printed and bound in China

20 19 18 17 16
10 9 8 7 6 5 4 3 2 1

Library of Congress Cataloging-in-Publication Data
Hardback ISBN 978 1 5157 2531 2
e-book ISBN 978 1 5157 2554 1

Acknowledgments
The author and publisher are grateful to the following for permission to reproduce copyright material: Getty
Images pp. 23 (Leemage), 24 (De Agostini / C. Sappa); Rex Features p. 19 (Eye Ubiquitous/REX Shutterstock);
Shutterstock pp. 1 (Vladimir Wrangel), 4 (Efremova Irina), 5 (WitR), 6 (Cornfield), 7 (Pius Lee), 10
(Mountainpix), 11 (Nagib), 12 (Nestor Noci), 14 (PRILL), 17b (Alfredo Cerra), 20 (Vladimir Wrangel), 21
(Malchus Kern), 22 (Dr Ajay Kumar Singh), 27 (Nomad_Soul), 29 top (Kokhanchikov); Wellcome Images cover
(Science Museum, London), p. 17 top (Science Museum, London); Wikimedia Commons pp. 8 (Carsten Frenzl
from Obernburg, Deutschland), 9 (Keith Schengili-Roberts), 13 (Walters Art Museum. Acquired by Henry Walters,
1927), 15 (Courtesy of Harrogate Museums and Arts), 18 (The Yorck Project), 25 (D. Denisenkov), 26 (Walters
Art Museum. Acquired by Henry Walters, 1909), 29 bottom (© Hans Hillewaert).

CONTENTS

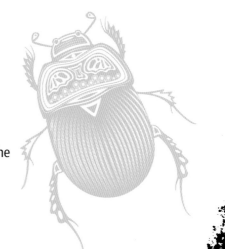

Throughout the book you will find Deadly
Secrets boxes that show an historical object.
Use the clues and the hint in these boxes to
figure out what the object is or what it was
used for. Then check out the Answer box at the
bottom of the page to see if you are right.

ANCIENT EGYPT

The Nile River flows through Egypt, creating a strip of **fertile** land through the sandy desert. People have lived there for thousands of years, and it was home to the **civilization** of ancient Egypt.

People started to settle along the edge of the Nile River about 8,000 years ago. They farmed the land and raised animals for food. The villages were clustered into two main groups: one in the south (called Upper Egypt) and one in the north (called Lower Egypt).

Egypt United

In about 3100 BCE, Upper and Lower Egypt were united under a single king. This was the start of a period lasting more than 3,000 years, in which kings and queens ruled Egypt. During this time, the Egyptian civilization became very powerful.

The Egyptian civilization depended on the water of the Nile River.

The enormous **pyramids** of Giza, near modern Cairo, were built during the Old Kingdom period (see below).

The ancient Egyptians built grand **temples**, palaces, and monuments. They also developed one of the world's first systems of writing and devised elaborate **rituals** for honoring and burying their dead. Although we know a lot about their rulers, most ancient Egyptians were ordinary people. They farmed, built houses, looked after their families, and served the king.

Egypt Conquered

In the sixth century BCE, the Persians conquered ancient Egypt, followed later by Alexander the Great. Finally, in 31 BCE, ancient Egypt became part of the mighty Roman **Empire**.

Secrets of the Dead

Egyptian Timeline

ca. 3100 BCE	Upper and Lower Egypt unite under King Narmer
ca. 2649–2150 BCE	The Old Kingdom: many pyramids are built
ca. 2040–1640 BCE	The Middle Kingdom: a peaceful time of great creativity
1552–1069 BCE	The New Kingdom: ancient Egypt becomes large and powerful
525 BCE	The Persians take over
332 BCE	Alexander the Great (from Macedon, northern Greece) takes over
31 BCE	Egypt becomes part of the Roman Empire

DIGGING UP THE PAST

For a long time, ancient Egyptian **culture** was a mystery to modern people. They could see the remains of ancient monuments, such as temples and pyramids. However, because they could not read the Egyptian picture writing, it was hard to find out about the world of the ancient Egyptians.

Everything changed when the ancient Egyptian **hieroglyphic** writing system was deciphered in the early 1800s. A huge amount of ancient Egyptian writings exist. **Archaeologists** are now able to read it to learn more about the history and culture of ancient Egypt.

There are still archaeological digs in operation all over Egypt, including this one near the Valley of the Kings.

Treasure Hunters

A long time ago, when wealthy Europeans visited Egypt as tourists, they often took home **artifacts**—carvings, jewelry, and even **mummies**—as souvenirs. In the early 1800s, several French archaeologists studied Egyptian monuments. By the end of the nineteenth century, many professional archaeologists were **excavating** in an orderly fashion. They kept records and made important new discoveries. Everything, from pieces of broken pottery to grand temples, increased our knowledge of ancient Egypt.

Finding Tombs

More and more **tombs** were found. They belonged to **pharaohs**, nobles, and even commoners. Nearly all the royal tombs had been robbed, sometimes thousands of years earlier. However, other tombs were filled with artifacts. The finding of the pharaoh Tutankhamun's tomb in 1922 was important because there were still so many precious items in it. Studying burials, as well as writings, art, and other artifacts, has given us a clearer picture of this amazing civilization.

Secrets of the Dead

The Sphinx

The Great **Sphinx** of Giza is one of ancient Egypt's most recognizable monuments. It was built more than 4,500 years ago. It shows the body of a lion with the head of a man. Most of its body was carved directly out of natural limestone. Many archaeologists believe that the face is that of Khafre, a pharaoh from the Old Kingdom, but no one knows for sure.

The limestone Sphinx sculpture at Giza is more than 65.6 feet (20 meters) high in places.

PHARAOHS: RELIGIOUS AND POLITICAL LEADERS

For much of its history, a single king-like ruler, called a pharaoh, ruled ancient Egypt. People thought he was a god living on Earth. They believed that pharaohs had magical powers. There were hundreds of pharaohs throughout ancient Egypt's history. Some of them had an enormous impact.

The pharaoh was a religious leader as well as a political leader. He would choose sites for temples and lead important ceremonies. He also made the laws, collected taxes, and led his country in war.

Tutankhamun was pharaoh for only about 10 years. He is famous because of the rich treasures found in his tomb, such as this mask that covered his head and shoulders.

Passing Down the Title

The title of pharaoh usually passed from father to son. Some pharaohs would name an **heir** instead. Pharaohs were very concerned about keeping the job of pharaoh in their own family. Many pharaohs married their sisters or half-sisters. One pharaoh even married his own daughters! In art, pharaohs are often shown holding a crook (a stick curved into a hook at one end) and a flail (like a whip). The crook symbolizes the pharaoh's role as protector of his people. The flail symbolizes punishment of his enemies.

DEADly Secrets

This is a statue of one of Egypt's pharaohs, Hatshepsut. Hatshepsut was a famous female pharaoh. There is something a little odd about it. Can you guess what it is?

Hint: It has something you would not normally expect to see on a woman's face.

Secrets of the Dead

Famous Pharaohs

Name	Reign	Claim to Fame
Narmer	ca. 3100 BCE	First king of the united Egypt
Khufu	2551–2528 BCE	Built the Great Pyramid of Giza
Khafre	2520–2494 BCE	Built pyramid at Giza; Sphinx may be a portrait of him
Hatshepsut	1490–1468 BCE	Female pharaoh who traded with people far away
Akhenaten	1364–1347 BCE	Pharaoh who introduced the worship of one god: Aten
Tutankhamun	1347–1337 BCE	Son of Akhenaten. His tomb was discovered in 1922
Ramesses II	1289–1224 BCE	One of the longest-reigning pharaohs
Cleopatra	51–30 BCE	Last queen of Egypt before it became a Roman province

Answer: The statue shows a pharaoh with a beard! Nearly all pharaohs were men but Hatshepsut was a woman. Most pharaohs were clean-shaven but they wore fake braided beards to look like the god Osiris. Hatshepsut was no different.

HARD WORKERS AND
BRAVE SOLDIERS

For much of its history, ancient Egypt depended on the hard work of its people. There were times when people had to spend a few weeks each year working for the pharaoh. They often worked on large-scale projects such as building pyramids. After they had finished, they were free to go back to their farms.

The work of laborers was one thing that kept ancient Egypt going. Another was the army. During the Old Kingdom, there was no national army, only small bands of fighters that the king could call on when needed. Archaeologists believe that in the Middle Kingdom, a full-time army was formed, although it was still small.

Low-ranking Egyptian soldiers like these would have been paid in bread and beer.

Army Life

- Roles ranged from high-ranking generals down to **logistics**, delivering supplies to the soldiers.
- Trumpeters and flag bearers helped keep troops organized during battle.
- When not fighting, soldiers would practice **maneuvers** or work on government projects, such as digging **canals**.
- Rewards for bravery included gold pendants in the shape of flies, which could be attached to necklaces.

Big and Powerful

In the New Kingdom period, ancient Egypt fought many wars. The army became much more important. At some times, soldiers from other lands, such as **Nubia** or Greece, were paid to fight in the Egyptian army. The army became well organized. Its commander-in-chief was the pharaoh.

Deadly Weapons

Ancient Egyptian soldiers fought with bows and arrows, bronze-tipped spears, and a type of curved sword called a "khopesh." They used shields made of wood or leather. In later periods, they wore simple armor of leather and metal. Elite troops fought in fast, maneuverable war **chariots**. Horses pulled these chariots. Each chariot carried two men: one to drive and one to fight.

It would have been difficult to shoot accurately from a fast-moving chariot!

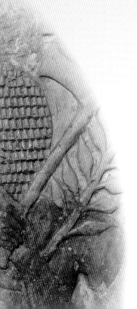

MANY GODS AND GRAND TEMPLES

Ancient Egyptian religion was complicated. There were many gods and goddesses and beliefs. The gods controlled different aspects of life. Some gods were worshiped only in certain places. They were worshiped in temples, where people thought the gods lived.

The most important god was Ra, the sun god. His descendants included Osiris, the god of the dead; Horus, a god of the sky; Anubis, god of **embalming**; and Set, the god of chaos. Many of the Egyptian gods and goddesses were related. Sometimes they fought with each other. Many were often shown as human bodies with the head of an animal.

The Egyptians sometimes mummified crocodiles. They left them as offerings for the crocodile-headed god Sobek. Sobek was associated with the Nile.

Temples and Worship

Most ancient Egyptian temples had a similar layout. There was a main gate leading into a courtyard. Beyond the courtyard, there were dark halls with tall columns and a sanctuary with a statue of the god. Only kings and priests were allowed inside the temple. Each day, the priests bathed and dressed the statue of the god. They gave him offerings of food.

Villages and homes had small **shrines** where the gods could be worshiped. Here, many people would worship lesser gods, such as Bes. Bes protected children and the home. The ancient Egyptians believed that signs, such as shooting stars and dreams, could be messages from the gods. They wore charms, called **amulets**, to ward off bad luck.

DEADly Secrets

This is one of the most popular styles of amulet in ancient Egypt. Can you guess what it shows?

Hint: It is the body part of a god.

Secrets of the Dead

Egyptian Gods: the Facts

God or Goddess	Animal Head	God of...
Anubis	jackal	embalming
Hathor	cow	love and joy
Horus	falcon	the sky
Khepri	scarab beetle	sunrise
Khnum	ram	flooding
Sekhmet	lioness	war
Sobek	crocodile	water
Thoth	ibis	writing and knowledge

Answer: This symbol is called the "eye of Horus." When he was fighting the god Set, Horus lost an eye but the god Thoth healed him. His eye became a symbol of healing. It was thought to bring good health.

DEATH
AND THE AFTERLIFE

Death was never far away for the ancient Egyptians. Without modern medicine, minor diseases and injuries could prove fatal. Many people died before the age of 30. Perhaps because of this, ancient Egyptians spent a lot of time thinking about and preparing for their next life after death.

They believed that after death, they still needed a body in order to live again in a new life. This is why the ancient Egyptians went to such lengths to preserve a person's body after he or she died. Using a process called mummification, the embalmers prepared the bodies for burial.

Many Egyptian tombs, like these ones, were cut into solid rock but ordinary people had simpler graves.

Tombs

Once a body was prepared for burial, it could be laid in a tomb. Tombs for ordinary people were often made of brick. Some early pharaohs were buried in giant pyramids. Later pharaohs were buried in tombs cut out of the rock. A priest would perform a special ceremony to prepare the body for the journey to the afterlife. A person's family would place things in the tomb that the dead person might need in the afterlife. This might include food, cooking equipment, jewelry, clothing, and furniture.

DEADly Secrets

This small figurine of a person was found in an Egyptian tomb. Many tombs had similar figures —sometimes dozens in the same tomb. What do you think it was for?

Hint: It was meant to serve the dead person. ••

Secrets of the Dead

The Weighing of the Heart

The ancient Egyptians believed that after death, the god Anubis would place a person's heart on a set of scales. Anubis would weigh the heart against the "feather of truth" (an ostrich feather). If the person had led a good life, the heart would be as light as the feather. He or she could pass into the next world and live there happily ever after. If the heart was heavy with sin, a monster would eat it and the person would be restless forever.

Answer: This figurine is a ushabti. It represents a servant. The ancient Egyptians thought that they might need to do work in the afterlife, so they placed ushabtis in a person's tomb to do the work for them. The richer you were, the more ushabtis you might have.

AMAZING MUMMIES AND CANOPIC CLUES

The ancient Egyptians believed that a human spirit could survive only if the body was preserved.

They used the process of embalming to keep bodies from rotting. If a body is not embalmed, digestive juices and bacteria rot the soft tissues, such as the skin and muscles. Only a skeleton would remain, and that was not good enough for the ancient Egyptians. The mummification process they invented was able to keep a body from rotting away.

Secrets of the Dead

How the Ancient Egyptians Made Mummies

- A long metal hook was put into the nose and the brain was pulled out and thrown away.
- The abdomen was cut open. The lungs, liver, stomach, and intestines were removed and saved.
- The body was covered in salty natron powder and left to dry for 40 days.
- The chest cavity was stuffed with rags and even sawdust, and a wig and makeup was added to make the body look as lifelike as possible.
- The body was wrapped in long linen strips.
- The body was placed in a wooden coffin. Some coffins were then placed inside a stone box called a sarcophagus.
- The tomb was filled with grave goods, then sealed.

Preparing for the Afterlife

When a body was mummified, important organs were kept in containers called canopic jars. But not the brain. The ancient Egyptians did not think it was important, so they threw it away. When the body was wrapped in linens, amulets were placed between the layers to protect the body in its journey through the underworld. Priests read out spells to ward off evil spirits.

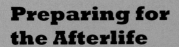

This limestone jar has a removable lid. It was found in an Egyptian tomb. Archaeologists believe it was made by a skilled craftsman around 3,700 years ago. What do you think might be inside?

Hint: It might be a little smelly by now!

Even today, 4,000-year-old Egyptian mummies still have skin, flesh, and hair.

Answer: This is a canopic jar, containing the stomach of the tomb's owner. The lid of the jar is the clue: it is shaped like a jackal. The jackal-headed Duamutef was the guardian of the stomach.

THE FLOODING RIVER AND PLANTING CROPS

Ancient Egypt was once described as "the gift of the Nile." This is because every year, the Nile River burst its banks and flooded the land. As the river went back to normal, it left behind a "gift" for the ancient Egyptians. This was a deep layer of fertile black soil in which farmers grew their crops.

The farmers had **irrigation** systems to water their crops. They dug networks of canals from the Nile River to their fields. The government made sure that the canals were kept in good condition. In later times, a machine called a "shaduf" was used to lift water from the canals to water the crops.

Main Crops

The most important crops for ancient Egyptian farmers were grains: barley and a type of wheat called emmer. Many farmers grew a plant called flax. Its fibers were used to make linen. Farmers also grew vegetables, fruits, and pulses. They often grew more than they could eat themselves. Some of the extra crops were paid in tax to the pharaoh.

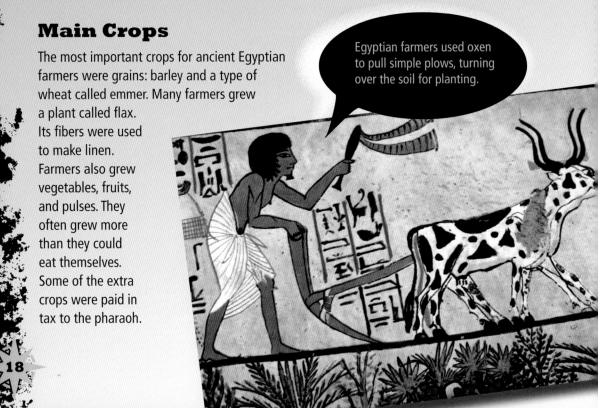

Egyptian farmers used oxen to pull simple plows, turning over the soil for planting.

A shaduf is a long lever with a bucket at one end for lifting water. The pole turns so that the bucket can swing around and be emptied where water is needed.

Livestock

There was a lot of fertile land so farmers used what there was for growing crops instead of grazing animals. However, many farmers kept sheep, goats, pigs, ducks, and pigeons. Oxen were used for pulling plows. Only rich people could afford to keep cattle for milk and beef. The ancient Egyptians used as much of an animal as they could. They drank the milk, ate the meat, and turned hides into leather and the bones into needles, bracelets, and rings. They burned the dung as fuel.

Secrets of the Dead

The Farming Calendar

The Egyptians divided the year into three seasons, each of which was divided into four months:

- Akhet (**inundation**—June to September): The time when the Nile flooded and the fields were underwater.
- Peret (growth—October to January): The time when crops were planted and left to grow.
- Shemu (harvest—February to May): The time when crops were harvested.

IMPORTANT JOBS AND BUSY TRADERS

Many of the ancient Egyptians were farmers. There were other important jobs, too. From high-ranking priests and government advisors to bakers and builders, there was a job for everyone.

The pharaoh needed thousands of people to help run the country. He had tax collectors to make sure that everyone paid their fair share. Officials kept track of the country's food supply. There were architects and engineers. They planned and carried out building work on temples, tombs, and other projects. There were also lawyers and judges to conduct trials.

The **scribes** wrote down everything and kept records. Being a scribe was a respected profession. Some scribes rose to become government ministers.

DEADly Secrets

These may look like rocks but they are not. This substance is not found naturally in Egypt. It was imported from hundreds of miles away. Can you guess what it is?

Hint: The Three Wise Men would have known what it was.

Craftspeople and Traders

Ancient Egypt's skilled artists and craftspeople made beautiful objects. Many of their materials came from other lands. Ancient Egypt **exported** grain and **papyrus** and in return, the ancient Egyptians were able to import (buy in) materials such as copper, timber, silver, and ivory.

Answer: These are lumps of myrrh. Myrrh is a type of hardened sap from trees. It was imported from the land that is now Somalia. It was very valuable. The ancient Egyptians burned myrrh for its smell. They also used it in the embalming process.

Secrets of the Dead

Deir el-Medina

In the nineteenth century, archaeologists discovered the village of Deir el-Medina. For about 500 years during the New Kingdom period, this village was home to the workers who built the nearby royal tombs. Stonecutters, sculptors, and painters all lived there, along with their families. The village is very well preserved, and it has shown us a lot about what daily life was like for ordinary people.

EATING, DRINKING, AND HUNTING

The grains grown by the farmers were the main food source for most ancient Egyptians. They made the barley and wheat into flour for bread and cakes, and also a weak, soupy beer. The water from the river and canals was not always clean enough to drink, so beer was much safer—even for children.

Poor people in ancient Egypt did not often eat meat. Beans and lentils provided their **protein**. They ate vegetables such as onions, leeks, radishes, and cabbage. Figs, dates, grapes, apples, pomegranates, and other fruits were also eaten. Honey was used to sweeten food. Many people drank milk. Milk went bad quickly in the heat. It was made into a yogurt-like food that kept longer.

Food for the Rich

Rich people had a more varied diet than poor people. They could afford to eat meat such as poultry and beef. They ate a wide variety of fruit and vegetables. They also drank wine, which was imported in the early days.

Dates grow in huge bunches on some types of palm trees. They are still a popular food in Egypt today.

Hunting and Fishing

In ancient Egypt, fishing and farming were important ways of obtaining food. However, some rich people saw hunting as a sport, and would go on hunting trips for fun. They hunted waterbirds, such as ducks and geese, as well as larger animals like rabbits, gazelles, and antelopes. They would even take on lions, crocodiles, hippos, and other dangerous animals.

Hunting waterbirds was a popular pastime. This man, known as Nebamun, is holding a throwing stick, which he would throw at the birds as they tried to fly away.

Cooking Outdoors

It is very hot in Egypt so in most ancient Egyptian homes, the kitchen was outside. It was either in a corner of a courtyard or on the roof of the house. Food could be cooked in a clay oven or over an open fire. Ancient Egyptian cooks had salt and a variety of spices and herbs such as cumin and coriander for flavoring. Food was usually served in clay dishes and eaten with the fingers.

WOMEN'S RIGHTS AND BUSY CHILDHOODS

Families were important in ancient Egypt. The father was the head of the family. Pharaohs often had several wives but most ordinary men had only one. Men would usually get married around the age of 20. Women married much younger —sometimes as young as 14.

This wall painting shows a man named Debu Sobek and his family.

Egyptian Women

Most women in ancient Egypt stayed at home, looking after the house and the children. However, they had more rights than women in some other ancient civilizations. They were allowed to own property, carry out business deals, and be witnesses in court. It was not unusual for a woman to run her husband's business when he was away. Some women from the middle and upper classes may have been able to read and write, although only men were allowed to be scribes.

The ancient Egyptians played a board game called senet. In it, pieces had to pass each other in order for a player to win.

A Child's Life

An Egyptian child would stay close to his or her mother for the first few years. A mother would often carry her baby around with her in a soft sling. Parents used amulets and prayers to protect their children but many children died young—only about half lived to adulthood.

In poorer families, children started to help out at home as soon as they were old enough. Boys were usually taught their father's trade. Girls learned from their mother how to cook, clean, weave, and sew. Boys from rich families would have school lessons. There, they would learn reading, writing, and mathematics.

Secrets of the Dead

Slavery in Egypt

For many centuries, **slavery** in the way that we normally think of it was very rare in ancient Egypt. In the later periods, foreigners who were captured in battle were sometimes brought to ancient Egypt to be used as slaves. A slave might work as a servant or a nanny, or work the fields on a farm. Many slaves were well treated.

SIMPLE CLOTHES AND BEAUTIFUL JEWELRY

So many carvings and paintings survive from ancient Egypt that we know a lot about what people wore. There are even rare examples of actual clothes, wigs, and shoes. People also wore jewelry and ornaments.

DEADly Secrets

This woman is wearing a wig but can you see the cone shape at the top? This is a lump of fat. At parties, both men and women would have one. What do you think it is?

Hint: It probably smells better than it looks! •••••••••••••••

> The man in this painted carving could be a pharaoh as he is wearing an elaborate headdress usually worn by pharaohs.

Lovely Linen

Most clothes were made from linen, a fabric woven from the fibers of the flax plant. Men wore a simple **kilt** made from a piece of linen wrapped around the waist and tucked in. Their chests were bare. Women wore a dress that came to their ankles, with shoulder straps at the top. In cold weather, both men and women might have worn linen cloaks. Rich people had more elaborate versions of the same thing, using thin, fine linen. In later periods, clothes made from pleated linen became fashionable. People either wore leather sandals or went barefoot.

Secrets of the Dead

A Guide to Hairstyles

DO keep your hair short if you are a man.

DO NOT shave your son's head but leave a ponytail on one side (called the "sidelock of youth").

DO be creative with hairstyles. Women can leave their hair loose or braided and decorate it with flowers and beads.

DO NOT forget to wear a fancy wig when you go to a party (this goes for both men and women).

Jewelry

Jewelry was popular in ancient Egypt but only rich people could afford items made from gold or precious stones. Poorer people had jewelry made from cheaper materials such as copper, beads or "faience" (blue or green paste made from **quartz** sand). Many people wore amulets for luck, as well as necklaces, bracelets, and big decorative collars.

Answer: Many archaeologists believe that the object is a lump of fat with perfume mixed into it. In the heat of the party, the fat would slowly melt and drip down into the wig. The perfume would keep the wearer smelling fresh.

WRITING BY PICTURES AND THE ROSETTA STONE

The ancient Egyptians developed one of the world's first systems of writing. They left behind a lot of written material. Everything, from histories, stories, and prayers to personal letters and lists of trade goods were written down or carved in stone.

Important messages were carved in stone using hieroglyphs. A lot of everyday writing was done on a form of paper called papyrus. Papyrus is a type of reed that grows along the Nile. Its stems were cut into strips and soaked, then formed into a flat sheet. A scribe would use a pen made from a reed to write on the papyrus with ink.

Understanding the Egyptians

Deciphering hieroglyphs, the ancient Egyptian system of picture writing, helped archaeologists understand this ancient culture. By reading official records, they have been able to figure out the history of the pharaohs and understand how they ran the country.

Secrets of the Dead

Hieroglyphs: the Facts

- This writing system was developed more than 5,000 years ago.
- There are more than 700 different signs, including people, objects, and animals.
- Many pictures stand for an actual object, and some can represent a sound.
- Hieroglyphs can be written from top to bottom, right to left, or left to right.

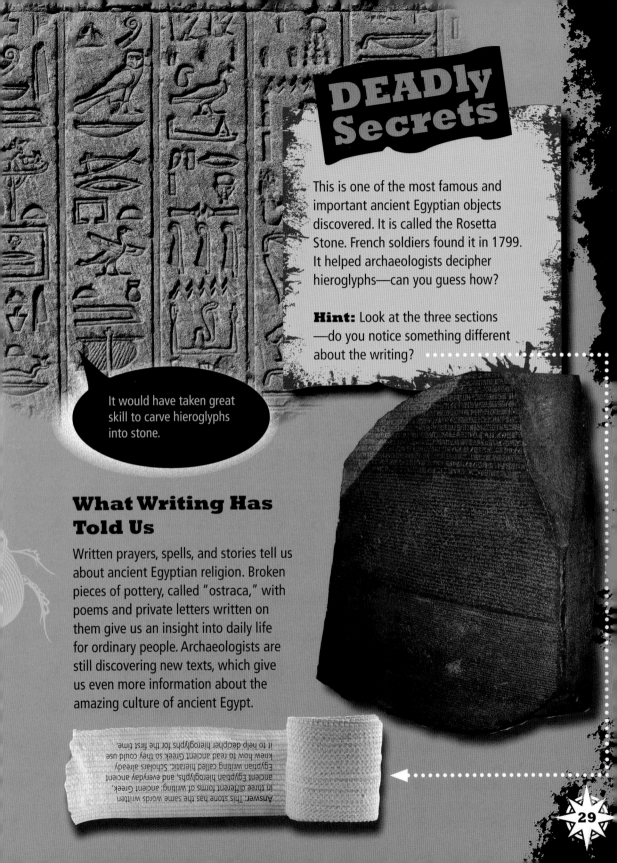

DEADly Secrets

This is one of the most famous and important ancient Egyptian objects discovered. It is called the Rosetta Stone. French soldiers found it in 1799. It helped archaeologists decipher hieroglyphs—can you guess how?

Hint: Look at the three sections—do you notice something different about the writing?

It would have taken great skill to carve hieroglyphs into stone.

What Writing Has Told Us

Written prayers, spells, and stories tell us about ancient Egyptian religion. Broken pieces of pottery, called "ostraca," with poems and private letters written on them give us an insight into daily life for ordinary people. Archaeologists are still discovering new texts, which give us even more information about the amazing culture of ancient Egypt.

Answer: This stone has the same words written in three different forms of writing: ancient Greek, ancient Egyptian hieroglyphs, and everyday ancient Egyptian writing called hieratic. Scholars already knew how to read ancient Greek so they could use it to help decipher hieroglyphs for the first time.

GLOSSARY

amulet small item worn for good luck or to ward off evil

archaeologist person who digs up and studies the remains of ancient cultures

artifact object made by a human being that has cultural or religious importance

canal long, narrow channel, dug to supply fields and crops with water

chariot two-wheeled carriage pulled by horses

civilization society, culture, and way of life of a particular area

culture ideas, beliefs, values, and knowledge shared by a particular group of people

embalming art of treating a dead body with chemicals to keep it from decaying

empire collection of territories ruled by an emperor or pharaoh

excavate uncover something buried by digging away the earth that covers it

export send goods to be sold in another country

fertile rich and good for growing crops

heir next in line to be king or pharaoh

hieroglyphic writing system based on pictures that represent a word, part of a word, or a sound

inundation flooding

irrigation artificial system of bringing water onto fields to help crops grow

kilt type of skirt that can be worn by men

logistics detailed planning and organizing

maneuvers moves

mummy body that has been embalmed and wrapped in linen in preparation for burial

Nubia ancient region of Northeast Africa, on the Nile, extending from Aswan to Khartoum

papyrus tall plant with stalks that can be used to make a type of paper that is also called papyrus

pharaoh Egyptian king

protein substance found in foods such as meat, eggs, and beans that people need to be healthy

pyramid large structure that has a square base and four triangular sides

quartz colorless mineral found in certain kinds of rock

ritual action or set of actions done over and over again for a special purpose, often connected to a person's religion

scribe person whose job is reading and writing

shrine sacred place devoted to honoring a god

slavery owning someone else and forcing them to work without pay

sphinx imaginary creature with the body of a lion and the head of a person

temple building where gods and goddesses are worshiped

tomb building or space above or below the ground where a dead body is kept

READ MORE

Books

Boyer, Crispin. *Everything Ancient Egypt: Dig into a Treasure Trove of Facts, Photos, and Fun* (National Geographic Kids). Washington, D.C.: National Geographic, 2012.

Catel, Patrick. *What Did the Ancient Egyptians Do for Me?* (Linking the Past and Present). North Mankato, MN: Heinemann, 2011.

Senker, Cath, and Melvyn Evans. *Ancient Egypt in 30 Seconds: 30 Awesome Topics for Pharaoh Fanatics Explained in Half a Minute* (Children's 30 Seconds). Lewes, UK: Ivy Press, 2015.

Williams, Marcia. *Ancient Egypt: Tales of Gods and Pharaohs.* New York: Candlewick, 2013.

Web Sites

Use the menu at the left of this site to find facts, timelines, and games about ancient Egypt:
www.childrensuniversity.manchester.ac.uk/interactives/history/egypt

This web site has an interactive map and a quiz about the ancient Egyptians:
www.dkfindout.com/us/history/ancient-egypt

Learn how an Egyptologist has dug up clues about King Tut's life:
http://kids.nationalgeographic.com/explore/history/king-tut-ancient-egyptian-mysteries

The Smithsonian's web site on ancient Egypt includes interesting facts, videos, and maps:
www.mnh.si.edu/exhibits/eternal-life

INDEX